The Other Side

The Other Side

Poems by

Lynne Carol Austin

© 2025 Lynne Carol Austin. All rights reserved.
This material may not be reproduced in any form, published,
reprinted, recorded, performed, broadcast,
rewritten or redistributed without
the explicit permission of Lynne Carol Austin.
All such actions are strictly prohibited by law.

Cover design by Shay Culligan
Cover image by iStock Getty Image
Author photo by Katie Emanuelson Photography

ISBN: 978-1-63980-769-7

Kelsay Books
502 South 1040 East, A-119
American Fork, Utah 84003
Kelsaybooks.com

For my husband, Bob
and caregivers everywhere

*When we share our hardest moments
we give permission to others to be
their most authentic, vulnerable selves.*

—Cristina M. R. Norcross

Acknowledgments

My heart is open to caregivers everywhere for their strength, courage and tenacity. In my experience as my husband, Bob, faced illness and the fear of death, I concentrated on poetry for *The Other Side*. The simple truth is no one understands what we as caregivers go through. We are pulled into our loved one's emotional orbit. We experience fear of the unknown, loneliness, the extra workload, loss of our own interests and confusing emotions. My hope is these poems resonate with you, dear reader, so you feel understood and heard, even when your voice won't utter a sound. We are forever united in our struggles because we give of ourselves, while we love deeply. Please know you are not standing alone.

I am here, in part, because of the people who hold me up: my children, Jesica, Tim, Sarah, Chris and Matt, along with the editors and writing groups I belong to. Many thanks to all those talented people. I'd be remiss to not mention the poets in Wisconsin who have influenced me, Cristina M.R. Norcross, Susan Huebner, Marcia Marino, Jim Landwehr, Elizabeth Harrahy, and other far-reaching poets, John Roedel, Iain S. Thomas, Mary Oliver, and Nayyirah Waheed.

My gratitude to Karen Kelsay, Jenna Wray, Olivia Loftis, and all the staff at Kelsay Books, for bringing my poetry to life on these pages, and believing in this project.

My special thanks to the following publications, in which versions of these poems previously appeared:

Blue Heron Review: "We are Heavy, Dr. Adam," "With a Breath"

Contents

DIAGNOSIS

Rudderless	15
We Are Heavy, Dr. Adam	16
Another Trench	17
The Helper	18
Shapeshifter	19
The Ghost of Cancer	20
Gobble My Way to Numbness	21
Lost	22
Options	23
Hands in the Dirt	24

CHEMOTHERAPY

Tour of Our Future	27
We Notice	29
Mayo Clinic: Built on Sacred Land	30
That Moment	31
Guard at the Gate	32
Mind Games	33
Duct Tape, Too	34
Lycus	35
Full Grown	36
Clean It Up	37
Midpoint: Abated or Growing	38
Today's Joy	39
I Step Away	40
Turn Tail	42
A Koan	43
Unexpected	44
The Last Chemo	45

RADIATION

Photon Laser	49
Art as Healing	50
Greta Garbo Redux	52
Waiting Room Geometry	53
Icky Is Useful	54
Nighttime Wisdom	55
Really?	56
Misi Ziibi	57
With a Breath	58

RESURGENCE

It's All Right	61
Small Gains	62
Self-Preservation	63
A Glimmer	64
Linus and Me	65
This Titan	66
Symphony	67
Shadows	69
For You, Dear Reader	70

DIAGNOSIS

Rudderless

The doctor's office chair is a small boat
   tossing in a squall. I'm white knuckled
hearings words like
      abiraterone, docetaxel, lupron
         unlike familiar, prostate, cancer, metastasis

A second opinion, grasping, more
   tests, same results, spawning another
wave of his carping fatigue, that shares
      the bed with dark depression, a
         bone-breaking fragile ego, him
searching for someone to blame, or
      a bargaining chip to dampen anger

Worry slaps my face like icy rain
   my breath caught mid-inhalation
all life stops, but
      the circling of gulping questions

How do we get to the other side
   what will it look like
when we get there, and

      will we both survive

We Are Heavy, Dr. Adam

We watch your mouth
our eyes unblinking
You utter measured words, no use
our heads rotate, a tilt-a-whirl jumble
flicking off data
only hearing, *cancer*

You explain the edge of life—
How many times per day
do you wheel this burden into the room?
At the end of your shift, do our stares
of disbelief fall from your clothing
to shatter like glass on the floor?

Once out the door, do our
hundreds of questions take flight
like a murmuration of blackbirds?
Do you sling our bricks of sadness off
your burdened shoulders upon
approach to your car?

Can you shake us loose, the ones
whose face plow the ground
still clinging to your ankles? And lastly
as you turn on your ignition, do you know
how to empty yourself
of all of us?

Another Trench

This is new: a line between my eyes
a groove, a rut, from furrowed
eyebrows, pinching so tightly
I can't seem to stop the frown.

Discussions, decisions over
treatments with consequences, I
dramatize expectations, order myself
to be the linchpin, soldiering on
with a steel rod up my spine.

The enemy reads me well. Battle lines
drawn with precision, and no grace in
this raging war. My face is a map of
his illness—

it doesn't belong to me anymore.

The Helper

i didn't mean
to diminish you, the
independent and proud one
the take charge
don't tell me what to do
man, with metastatic cancer

it's only my worry, so leadened
i'm sinking to the bottom
my wringing hands want
action to accomplish, anything
so, i take over
many things, and hover
between an open door
and a closed door
not sure which side to stand on

Shapeshifter

If it looks like a duck
Swims like a duck
Quacks like a duck
Then it probably is a duck
  —18th-century idiom

I have sprout feathers
from shoulders to fingertips
so your steaming harsh words
no longer sear my skin
but slide off my plumage
into the mouth of the earth
to be swallowed, dissolved
forgotten

I repel like a duck

The Ghost of Cancer

The specter waits
riding the currents of our night-time breaths
standing with starving eyes, plate in hand
lurching close on our walks, counting
the steps to slice in and stand between us

His opportunity to ignite the burn . . .

  The myopic blame
    YOU did this!
  The strategic shame
    YOU didn't do that!

Greased expectations that crack our
spines and curl our lips, tears scorch
the earth so nothing takes sprout, no
green shoots flourish into sustenance

Fed up, I shout—
  I banish you from our kingdom!

The ghoul's hideous laugh echoes his reply
  We'll see . . .
      We'll see . . .

Gobble My
Way
to Numbness

To
Stuff
Fear
Banana Cream Pie
Worry
Salty Potato Chips
Anxiety
Chocolate Chip Cookies
Sadness
Rocky Road Ice Cream
Anger
Buttery Pop Corn

Unable to stop
Pushing it down

d
o
w
n
d
o
w
n

Inside

Lost

I'm the vessel for our fears
remembers for the two of us
performs functions you can't

until it's all too much

emptiness becomes me
a void for anger to fill
then—I don't recognize myself

I can't find my way back home

Options

If hope were a blue door
how soon would I
grasp the handle
to turn my suffering
into possibilities
of a new day rising
of eagles soaring
so high
my perspective
would lift me up to discover
many colored doors
each one hiding a threshold
to cross
options of my choosing
to live in a different way

Hands in the Dirt

the home for earthworm castings
decomposing leaves and plants
microbes, fungus, and grubs

searching roots spreading
clumps in need of kneading
soil blackens fingernail beds
and outlines my lifeline—
all of it, saves me

CHEMOTHERAPY

Tour of Our Future

In the distance—
brick and mortar buildings
clusters of mushrooms
rising from the ground, signals
the five hour drive complete

Inside Mayo Clinic—
the mycelium of
underground hallways
lead between numerous buildings
to the crème de la crème of healthcare

In the lobby—
imported wood and polished marble
highlight a winding staircase and two-story windows
a pianist strikes lilting notes on a grand piano
the Beatles love song "Here, There, Everywhere"

Dr. Kwon's office—
seventh floor elevator, but wait!
Detours of eye-pleasing artwork
here, there, everywhere: Anni Alder weaving
Andy Warhol lithographs, Dale Chihuly chandeliers

Waiting room thoughts—
Dr Kwon, *guru of prostate cancer,* meditate on
Kuan Lin, Buddhist deity of healing . . . *she
who harkens to the cries of the world*—
merge your knowledge and her energy

Hopeful outcome—
Dr. Kwon holds Kuan's vessel of healing, and
swings his sword to slay our dragon, with
his words: *we'll throw everything at this cancer*
but the kitchen sink—we'll throw the kitchen sink at it too!

will prove a fatal blow to all that is growing unchecked

We Notice

Waiting rooms display short-cropped
hair or no hair at all, baseball caps
pushing ears out with nowhere to go
skulls wrapped in silk flowered scarves
loudly colorful or modestly simple

Downcast eyes to avoid viewing
another's world of suffering, few
take the chance to smile, even less
to exchange conversation

The hallways bring couples holding
liver-spotted hands, pinched eyebrows
posing questions, or spouses walking
one ahead of the other, the attempt
to relieve their reality

But the sight that caused our stumble—
a mother's slamming heels and set jaw
pushing a wheelchair, the size engulfing
her child, with only the seven-year-old's
bald head uncovered by the rough white
hospital blanket, the pee-wee's
chin down, eyes closed

and our hearts cracked open

Mayo Clinic: Built on Sacred Land

in honor of the Dakota people

1.
The Peace Plaza. A reflecting pool, water fountain, hundreds of native words on stone pavers—*this is a Dakota place, the waterway our lifeway*—words of stardust, the Creator, ceremonies, obligation to live in harmony with the earth.

2.
The Original People asked, the plants responded: *use us for cancer,* said the chaga fungus on the birch tree, *and us for the lungs,* added mullein, willow and tamarack spoke, *we soothe arthritis.* The Wisdom Keepers learned. In the steel towers above, the doctors' memories fog.

3.
The Dakotas drumbeat pulses the heartbeat of the earth—never to keep silent. The ancestors' voices still alive under centuries of dirt. Their spirited vibration encircles, imploring us to listen; *it might not be too late.*

That Moment

the alarm in his voice
calls me to his side
he stands on the deck
legs spread wide

his voice, now whispers

    look

he reaches for the brim
lifting his baseball cap
a salute to the blue sky

snowflakes of white hair
spill, then swirl in the breeze
glint in the sunlight

  they are lost in space

seconds tick: we hold our gaze
understanding brings
moist eyes, tenderness
moves us into an embrace

my hand glides over the fabric of his
black shirt, sweeping to erase the
littered evidence of chemo
my absurd thought—

    now, this is real

Guard at the Gate

It is an unusual occurrence to witness two large red-tailed hawks parent their juvenile on the ground, as the hawk usually commands a higher perspective. Their tutelage attempts to corral him, their gait awkward while his movement is erratic and tipsy, wings arched for balance.

Once they are back in the trees, too close to the treasured wren nest, my love plays a recording of a hawk shriek. An attempt to establish dominance. But he plays a mating call. It attracts another hawk wanting to hook up with the, *come hither yoo-hoo.* Now, there are four hawks.

The next day, frantic cries of wrens jolt me, as I see a large shadow sail across the grass. I run out, clap my hands, and wish my voice could summon the inner bark of a baritone Labrador. I startle when four hawks explode from various trees, branches swinging, four-foot wingspans flapping. I remain watchful, repeat my exercise of interrupting natural selection.

My actions will crown me the neighborhood weirdo. I assume my neighbor is fogging up the window saying, *There she goes again.* But, the five wide-mouthed fuzzy-headed Jenny wren chicks need a chance. Just like my fuzzy-headed chemo husband needs me as his warrior.

Mind Games

Each phone conversation during
my respite, your voice, velvet smooth
lulled me into thinking
you were the man from two years ago

I visualized not the man of today—the
one battling chemo's relentless torment
but the one with tousled hair, joy in his
clear blue eyes, no hard lines in his face

Loss of the present left me unnerved
questioning how contact with reality
could be hijacked, blocked without
warning, lost in the unbound ethers

Or perhaps, it's simpler to admit my
desire to go back to easier times, before
our lives evolved into losing you
piece by piece

Duct Tape, Too

I hold it together
with safety pins or hair clips
using items from the junk drawer
rubber bands and thumbtacks
superglue unburied, usually
bone-dry

If one thing begins to slip
a dab of spackle or a stitch
needle and thread close by
patches too, but, nonetheless
an arsenal has been collected

Until someone asks
How are *you* doing?

The benevolent question
melts my mask, a softened
chin slides to my chest
with vulnerability revealed
tears drip onto my lap
as I step into my grief

Lycus

On all fours
fingernails pierce the soil
night's moisture lay upon me
moon's celestial glow aids instinct

the back arches
muscles lift in response
chin points skyward
throat elongates in readiness

to launch a frightful
burning howl from
the depth of
my wild

This woman's right
railing a haunting lament
bay and repeat
until all is exhausted

knowing the wolf and I
are sisters, relatives
in sharing
this shadowy darkness

this loneliness
here, now—
when all one can do
is howl

Full Grown

The unyielding ground bites into my knees.
Lately, no time for weeding or tenderness
to the flowers who give so much to
be noticed. I implore forgiveness and dig.

With my fist full of weeds comes their questions—
*How do you think you're doing? This is a
test for the one who calls herself spiritually minded.*

These thistle remarks prick.

Sitting back on my haunches, with crow in
my mouth, admit, I've only earned a C.
Too many complaints of piled-on work
focusing on the negative.

I whine, *Cancer is the puppeteer.* I'm the marionette
jumping at every jerk, wearing a wooden smile.

Burrowing deeper, they ask—
How far have you fallen?

What arises is a holy desire to find me again!
To open my heart to a more kind, loving version.

They say, *It might take everything you've got.*

This Queen of Hearts knows they are right
but still yells, *Off with their heads!*

Clean It Up

after Iain S. Thomas, "A Door Slammed Off Its Hinges"

Maybe the mess of you
is reflected
in the mess of me

Let's find something
hilarious to laugh about
weep and drip snot

We can be a mess
of a different sort
then our other mess
might not seem so bad

Midpoint: Abated or Growing

Hanging.
Hanging on depends on how you
see the world. The weight of hope
hanging by the thinnest of threads, or
hope harnessed—a stallion ready to
gallop the open plains.

Sleep.
Sleep depends on hope. Only the mind
is determined hope is the stallion and
you're ready to ride all night. Sleep decides
to hang precariously, tells the body to
toss and turn.

The doctor.
The doctor has slept soundly. He has the
answers of hanging on and hope. He enters
smiles, and pumps my husband's hand
like he just won a race. *Continue your chemo
all the lesions are not showing up!*

Surprise.
Surprise is a funny thing. A different kind
of hanging, suspended in space, and forgets
about hope. Surprise makes you mute. You
question your hearing. The words float on
the surface, not willing to sink in.

And you ask,
Is happiness always a guarded pursuit?

Today's Joy

It may only be
a fleeting moment
a butterfly's delicate
flirt onto a flower stamen

looking to powder her nose
in a yellow mist of pollen
then flit away
wings open and close

a thermal breath of
existence—reminding me
the joy of gentle flutters
can keep us alive

I Step Away

It is here—
In the forest, among the
sentinels of pine and birch
I telegraph my presence
greet them with my tender touch
the pine's rugged grooves and crags
sap dripping, or birches satin
paper skin, all accept me
as harmless.

My eyes search the pinnacles
of their crowns. I whisper,
Hello, Grandmother, to one
to another, *I see you, Grandfather.*
They sway to the salutation
these caretakers who provide
and fill my heart with
their grace.

It is here—
the dew moistens my shoes
wet soaking through to skin.
I practice my Fox Walk, the gentle
silent steps, in hopes any creature
will stop a moment to allow me
to take slow breaths
and stare.

It is here—
the sun filters through the leaves
spotlights the wildflowers of lily
violet and trillium. Some consider
plants I can't name, weeds
others may label them medicinal.
Someday, I will study
to learn them all.

For now, I merge with the forest
floor, pulsate with this living energy
celebrate the hues of green, from
celadon to holly, fill my lungs with
scents of pine, Sweet Fern, moss
and accept the forgotten nurturing
now relished.

Turn Tail

It was me people spoke of
in hushed tones, their
inflection not mocking
but wonderment—
is this courage or insanity
to uncross one's arms
spread them wide
run to a lift off
ascend with the crows
cackle with their caws
and circle the earth below
with abandoned perspective

where big things
look small
and small things
become invisible

A Koan

It takes a long time to understand nothing.
—Lucy to Charlie Brown

and nothing prepares us
for suffering

yet, my love has gathered
a lifetime of clowning silliness

and quick humor
to weaken suffering

in a duel of wit and comebacks
and a trail of one-liners, then

suffering becomes nothing—
or everything

Unexpected

we salute James Gardner, WWII parachute veteran

Three months to live, our neighbor, Jim, was told. It didn't stop
him and my love, Bob, from standing together, heads bent
sharing struggles, cancer treatments, fears: this boys club—
no girls allowed. Except one day.

I heard Bob say, *When my dad was dying, I told him I loved him.*
Dad said, 'Ah-huh.' Bob shrugged. *I know he loved me, but*
I needed to hear him say it. So, Jim, tell your kids
you love them.

Jim waved it away, explaining when his son declared his love
Jim was silent. He added, it was easier to tell his daughters.
It's a generational thing.
We never did that.

Bob said, *What! Your boys need to hear, 'I love you!'* A pause
then Bob's eyes sparkled with challenge.
I love you, Jim.

Jim stiffened. Eyes widened. Lips trembled. He swallowed hard.
I imagined his circuits popping. His standstill gave way to
I love you, Bob. Jim stretched taller. Our eyes met.
I love you, Lynne.

Three of us, hugs genuine. Tears mixed on wet cheeks.
As an interloper, I witnessed a most unexpected moment
of exquisite healing.

The Last Chemo

For years I've echoed the advice of experts. Eat fresh foods to avoid preservatives. Wash fruits and vegetables, to remove pesticides. Avoid foods with lectins, a protein that harms the gut lining. Limit sugar, artificial sweeteners, processed meats, which contribute to heart disease.

She sails into the cubicle, after donning a protective gown, wearing two pair of gloves, not one, but two, carrying a plastic bag labeled: HAZARDOUS DRUG . . . CAUTION. She reaches for your port, no longer a harbor of safety. Now the entrance of toxic waste to be introduced into your rivers and streams, to travel to every cell, welcomed or not. She smiles and is engaging, like all commercials trying to sell you cholesterol raising, oil laden, snack foods. But her snack has a punch.

You smile and joke. Our eyes meet across the room, conveying stoicism. We've agreed to this treatment plan, as upside down as it seems. They tell us your hair should grow back, your blackened toenails too. The fatigue will lessen and your energy will resume. The sores in your mouth will subside and your taste for food return. When that does, I will buy you cookies and donuts, and any other nasty food you are hungry for.

RADIATION

Photon Laser

May you not become a puddle
                          like the wicked witch of the west
Or open the ghostbusting gateway
                          to another dimension
But alter rogue cells, and beam up
                          in the most enterprising way

Art as Healing

Daniel Goldstein's kinetic mobile, Light on the Lake
—Mayo Clinic, Rochester, MN

Numerous turns down long hallways, trudging toward the
tattoo session for his oncology radiation, an atrium greets us
we blink at the brightness, and
notice a sense of
you have arrived

Across the expansive space, a thirty-foot mobile hangs from
the ceiling. Its intricacy halts my feet, raises my chin, my eyes
capture the glint of electric blues, welcoming us in artistic grace
awakening the senses
a must-do list can dull

A smile eases tension, appraising the layers of crescent shapes
there must be one thousand, each hanging by the thinnest of
threads, a cause for a spider to be enamored by
the complexity and
innate planning

With air movement, the shimmering crescents undulate a wave
impersonating the breath: inhalation and exhalation, softly
the ripples cross the sculpture
reminding me to breathe

Light from the two-story windows, reflect off the quarter moon
shapes, in azure, cerulean, cobalt blue: a painting by Monet, or
colors found in warm coastal water, and I remember the thunder
of the surf, the blow-away nothingness of the foam, while
the toes in my tight shoes curl
looking for warm sand

During my awed gaze, a spiritual awareness opens. We are
so suspended in this place between life and death, yet
securely held, the work toward healing continues in the
state of sacred light and
uncertainty of shadow

And what is the risk of prolonging life, but to
remember and practice deep-seated love
for ourself, along with each other
in the cherished
glittering moments left

Greta Garbo Redux

Scene I
She arrived at the hotel breakfast. She arrived two minutes before closing. Bleach blonde bed hair, neon against her full-length pink robe. Face free of makeup, but not cosmetic surgery. Slippers shuffled. Eyes searching. Coffee found. Her courage, interesting; my cereal, dull.

Scene II
We were statues seated in the oncology radiation waiting room. Heads turned. She floated above the floor. She was Greta Garbo from 1930s film noir. Her white, wool cape with dark fur trim, studio perfect, moved like silk. Her hair now styled. Fuchsia lipstick impeccable. Trepidation lay across her eyes. I wanted to hug her.

Scene III
At a change of hotels, the white, wool cape with dark fur trim draped over a luggage carrier, holding huge suitcases, numerous small bags. In my world of synchronicity why was she in my orbit? She strolled down the hall wearing a leopard skin duster. The calf of her tall boots, wider than her legs, slapped back and forth.

Scene IV
Another day. At the front desk, I spot her wearing a winter coat. The elbows worn to frayed rips. The same knee-high boots pulsing a beat as she walks. No longer Greta Garbo sweeping through a room. But her fuchsia lipstick—perfect.

Waiting Room Geometry

My eyes bounce along the parallel
lines of seats, occupied or empty, until
I am satisfied the number comes up
the same. Sixty chairs, not fifty-seven or
-eight. Sixty minutes since he went in
for his test.

Here, at the intersection of concern and
obsessiveness, I notice the geometric
fabric on the back of the blue chairs.
Twenty-three one-inch squares in a row
nineteen rows from top to bottom
tiny yellow circles in each square.

Multiplication for the sum of squares
and circles has my mind in a third-degree
rant. I silently scream, *What's the point!*
then angle my gaze toward
the opening door.

The wattage on his radioactive smile
gives me pause, but doesn't fool me.
I fake normalcy too
and return a relieved but much duller grin.

Icky Is Useful

The robins begin gathering
for fall migration, and
pending icky weather.
That's right, icky weather.

The five-year-old's word, *icky,* has
replaced descriptive words I have
command of. It pops out without
forethought, straight off the prize
shelf of a carnival game, pretty
and useful at first, but falls apart
soon after.

In my self-examination, my regression
of summoning *icky,* lifts me through
the clouds in a Ferris wheel basket
eye to eye with the birds. A safety net
of sorts. No need to plummet into
deeper emotions I have no fortitude
to deal with now.

Nighttime Wisdom

Favorite sleep positions forsake me. Clashing thoughts
become a bull elephant crashing through the bush. But
your reverie lifts me from the charge. I listen, along with
the silenced nighttime creatures.

   Who cooks for you . . . who cooks for you all

You materialize as if summoned, barred owl. Your primeval
call fills the black space with a halo of sound. I count seven
seconds between your hoots. The number indicates life shifts
and forthcoming revelations.

   Who cooks for you . . . who cooks for you all

Your astute yellow eyes perceive the enigmas of the
night. Are you here to unlock my tunnel vision, my
willful perceptions? Your neck turns in awareness
mine stiff, frozen in worry.

   Who cooks for you . . . who cooks for you all

A memory gently settles—a walk at dusk, an owl
sweeping down, his wingspan filled the path, and
silent flight guided me forward in quiet contemplation.
The same contemplation now.

   Who cooks for you . . . who cooks for you all

Great owl, you arrived as Spirit's blessing, to strike the
thought bubbles of conflict. To remind of natural order
while revealing the golden light of healing into
my brooding night.

Really?

A little more persistence, a little more effort, and what seemed hopeless failure may turn to glorious success.
—Elbert Hubbard

my fatigued
arms
are trembling
under
your weight
while
roiling seas
crest
over your
head
how long
can
i hold
you
up—or
am
i even
supposed
to try

Misi Ziibi

Algonquin words for "Big Water"

I've fallen out of myself
my tears of self-pity
join the course of the grand river

The mistress, in her silent command
carries my sighs, careening
over the washboard of flashing
jagged rocks, to finally meet
fallen golden leaves
in the swirl of an eddy

The churning motion rinses
the upstream concerns
distinguishes what is useful
to hold onto
and what belongs
swallowed and buried
in the thick sediment
of her graveyard

The seasoned river knows

With a Breath

You are not here without connections
the cording of love
braided strings to your heart
your breath, your very existence

Yet, when you lose your way
you wander, scissors in hand, ready
to cut the very union to the stars
the heavens
suffering because you think you must
allowing the seepage of your vital energy
holding against the intake of life

Until, we sweep you up into our wings
lifting your heaviness with ease
while breathing into your lungs
what you forgot you possessed all along

Hope

RESURGENCE

It's All Right

So, today you don't feel like being
that person: having the right soothing
words, acting responsible, greasing
all the cogs in the wheel.

Ask—*Who's showing up today?*

Then, let her out. Let her out to scream
in the closet, shimmy with the music
walk in the rain, cry with the gulls.

Otherwise, you'll be the person who wants
to run, but forgets to come back.

Small Gains

The peony bush is deer salad
some years able to blossom
most seasons scraggy branches
stripped of all leaves, except
one branch, a crooked finger
motions me forward

With pent-up emotions, I send
my shovel into the earth, and
struggle as the peony tubers fight
their release, careless words fill
the air, to finally face a vacant hole—
the emptiness gives me new options

Self-Preservation

I have become a cursive sentence
            where the letters d   dangerously
                        ip
                          below the line
  the haphazard loops are lopsided leaners, and
my dangli
        n
              g descenders plunge into letters below

where I forgot to dot the i's and cross the t's
        and the sentence threatens to
                  leave the page for insubordinat
                                  i
                             o
                                n

This disorder requires more than
        an eraser or wh teout, or a ruler
                  reminder to stay in the lines. It is a
finger-wagging warning to rewrite the
                        script for my self-worth—

    to turn the endless light I *shine* for others

  completely   o n
                  r   d
             a   to me

A Glimmer

The tune of who I am, written on
a single sheet of lined music paper
pinned down with a granite paperweight

A gentle breeze from the open window
ruffles the paper's edge, faking
the possibility of release

My grandchildren enter, all sparkles, and
curiosity of small hands lift the weight
I sigh, unencumbered

The Grands' giggles encourage the notes
to swell, and music pushes the boundary
of my lungs, like the first breath

Spirit unfurled, hands held, I sing the
song of hope, and we croon the melody
of awakened living

Linus and Me

There is safety in living small
only peeking at the brilliant sun
in hiding behind the door
when someone knocks, in
closing out the clamoring
circus band, that insists
accompaniment into the Big Top
in sheltering from the wind
retracting my turtle head, my
skin the boundary, my thoughts
contained within.

This is the house of my healing—
the solitude I need, the required
distance to breathe deep, and
slowly invite myself
to become whole again.

This Titan

It takes a mythical effort to hold up
the world, wearing an Atlas costume
crumbled paper to fill the biceps, along
with my quaking, thick thighs

What I didn't realize, is holding up
the spinning world creates a millstone
slowly grinding down onto bedstone
a crushing into flour

I'm told it might take months, maybe years
to find the right leavening agent to make me
rise again

Symphony

The worry of cancer is
pots and pans and lids and
metal spoons clanging to the
floor, deafening my inner

music, not just for a minute, but
holding the fermata, causing me
to forget the song given to me
at birth—
                I close my eyes
                welcome a different
                image and move formless
                into the woods, to

                walk with muted footsteps
                on last year's leaves, swing into
                a waltz under the towering
                pines, as the breeze caresses

                the pine needles into sighs
                together, we sigh, chuckle at the
                constant scolding chatter of the
                red squirrel, and watch the deer's

                amazing grace, only to hear the
                sweet sound of the songbirds
                conduct the forest in a tempo of
                all-is-right-with-the-world, and

like the rabbit frozen in place
my ears twitch and pitch
toward a distant beat—with
a realization the ancestors

are near, drumming the
heartbeat of the earth and
my heart beats in
universal soul music
                        Now, I remember my song

Shadows

There will come a time, when all of this
will be a story. We love stories, and
our suffering is validated when we
busy ourselves with the telling.

The stories mean it has happened in
the before, and once you tire of
retelling the telling, you'll have the
chance to move fully into
the light of living.

For You, Dear Reader

Through the uncertainty
the unveiling of truth
the waiting for options
the miracles alluded to
the losses chalked up
minor gains made

Understand—
a little light can
seep under a door

About the Author

Lynne Carol Austin lives in Wisconsin with her husband. She has four grown children and two grandchildren who are a source of delight. Austin is a member of Wisconsin Fellowship of Poets and The Wisconsin Writing Association.

She has published poetry in *Blue Heron Review* and *Wisconsin Poets' Calendar*; short stories in *Main Street Rag Literary Magazine*; a short story C.D., *Earth Spirituality*; three children's books, *Edith Ann Marie—The Sun Is In My Heart, Tell Me A Story Mama—Little Berry and Mama Bear,* and *Francine and Hazel*; two novels, *Ten of Swords* and *Gull Soup*. In her career as a registered nurse and alternative health practitioner, she published articles and chapters in alternative health magazines, along with a feature chapter in the book, *The New Healers—Minds and Hands in Complementary Medicine* by Dr. Barbara Stevens Barnum.

Find out more at:
www.lynnecarolaustin.com

www.ingramcontent.com/pod-product-compliance
Lightning Source LLC
Chambersburg PA
CBHW071332190426
43193CB00041B/1758